Piano/Vocal/Guitar

EVEN MORE SONGS of the FORTIES

THE DECADE SERIES

CONTENTS

ISBN 0-634-09118-2

HAL•LEONARD CORPORATION
7777 W. BLUEMOUND RD. P.O. BOX 13819 MILWAUKEE, WI 53213

D1571683

Visit Hal Leonard Online at
www.halleonard.com

A – YOU'RE ADORABLE

Words and Music by BUDDY KAYE,
SIDNEY LIPPMAN and FRED WISE

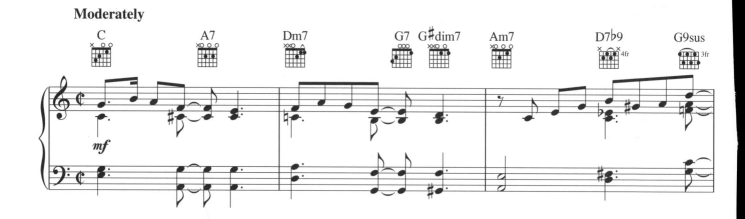

When John-ny Jones was ser-e-nad-ing Mar-y, he

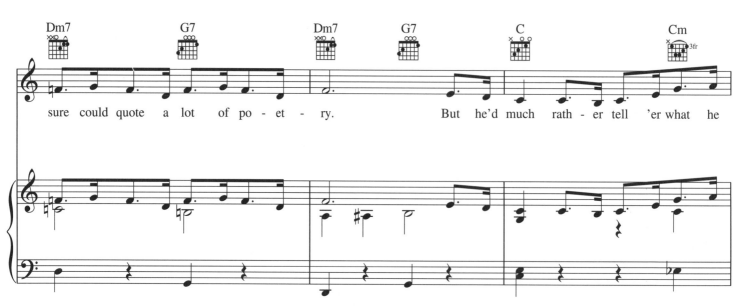

sure could quote a lot of po-et-ry. But he'd much rath-er tell 'er what he

ALL OR NOTHING AT ALL

Words by JACK LAWRENCE
Music by ARTHUR ALTMAN

10

ANGEL EYES

Words by EARL BRENT
Music by MATT DENNIS

AREN'T YOU GLAD YOU'RE YOU

Words by JOHNNY BURKE
Music by JIMMY VAN HEUSEN

BABY, IT'S COLD OUTSIDE

from the Motion Picture NEPTUNE'S DAUGHTER

By FRANK LOESSER

BÉSAME MUCHO
(Kiss Me Much)

Music and Spanish Words by CONSUELO VELÁZQUEZ
English Words by SUNNY SKYLAR

Bé - sa - me, ___ bé - sa - me mu - cho, ___
Bé - sa - me, ___ bé - sa - me mu - cho, ___

each time I cling to your kiss I hear mu - sic di - vine. ___
co - mo si fue - ra es - ta no - che la úl - ti - ma vez; ___

Bé - sa - me mu - cho, ___
bé - sa - me mu - cho, ___

26

DO YOU KNOW WHAT IT MEANS TO MISS NEW ORLEANS

Written by EDDIE DE LANGE
and LOUIS ALTER

I nev-er had this kind-a feel-in'

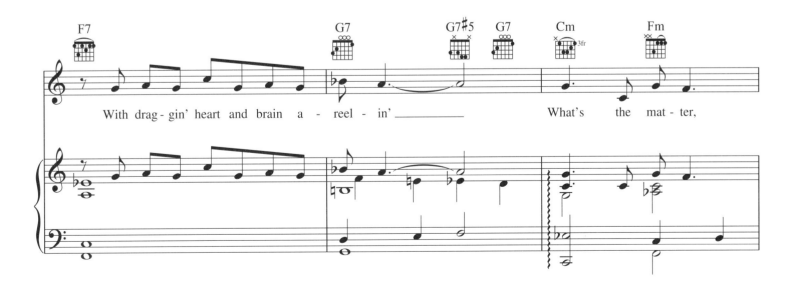

With drag-gin' heart and brain a-reel-in' _____ What's the mat-ter,

30

CALDONIA
(What Makes Your Big Head So Hard?)

Words and Music by
FLEECIE MOORE

Medium Boogie Woogie

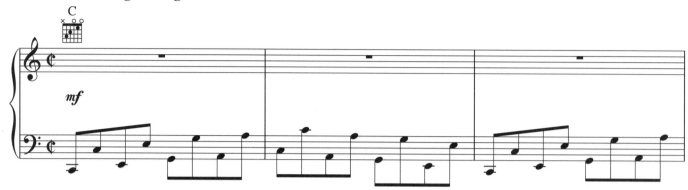

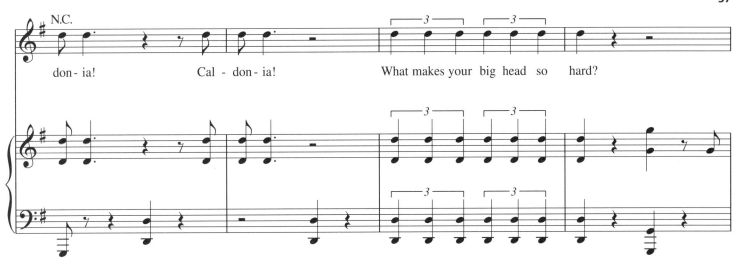

don - ia!   Cal - don - ia!   What makes your big head so   hard?

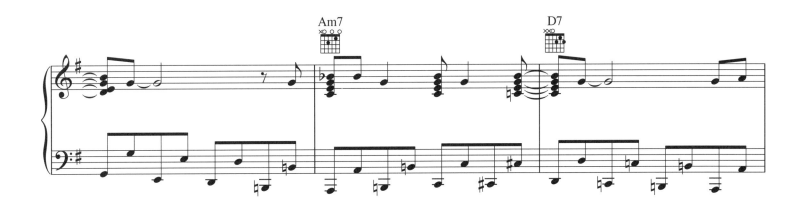

CHI-BABA CHI-BABA
(My Bambino Go to Sleep)

Words and Music by MACK DAVID,
AL HOFFMAN and JERRY LIVINGSTON

COMME CI, COMME ÇA

English Lyric by JOAN WHITNEY and ALEX KRAMER
French Lyric by PIERRE DUDAN
Music by BRUNO COQUATRIX

DADDY'S LITTLE GIRL

Words and Music by BOBBY BURKE
and HORACE GERLACH

Lit - tle girl of mine, with eyes of shin - ing

blue, lit - tle girl of mine, I love you, yes, I

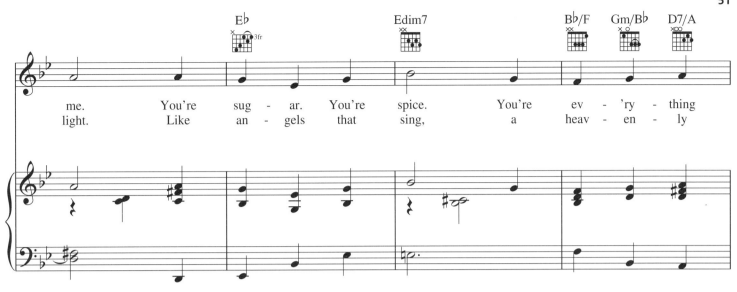

me.   You're   sug - ar.   You're   spice.   You're   ev - 'ry - thing
light.   Like   an - gels   that   sing,   a   heav - en - ly

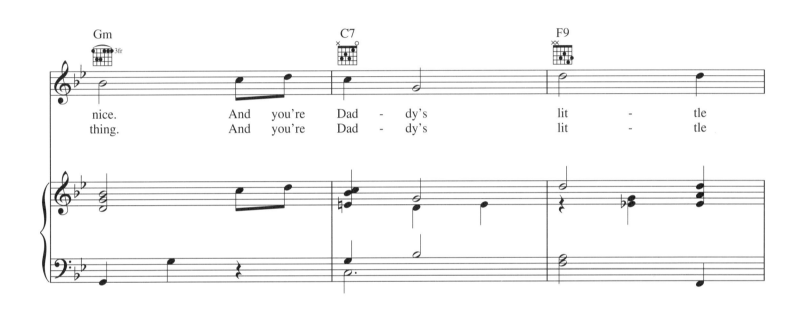

nice.   And   you're   Dad - dy's   lit - tle
thing.   And   you're   Dad - dy's   lit - tle

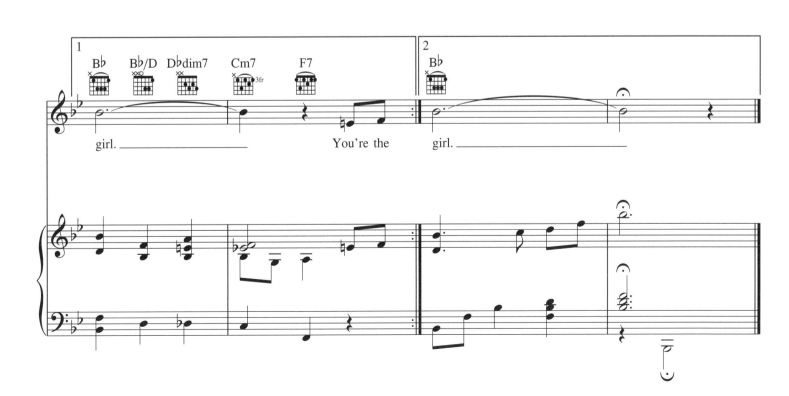

girl. _____   You're the   girl. _____

DON'T GET AROUND MUCH ANYMORE

from SOPHISTICATED LADY

Words and Music by DUKE ELLINGTON
and BOB RUSSELL

ELMER'S TUNE

Words and Music by ELMER ALBRECHT,
SAMMY GALLOP and DICK JURGENS

EARLY AUTUMN

Words by JOHNNY MERCER
Music by RALPH BURNS and WOODY HERMAN

Slowly, with feeling

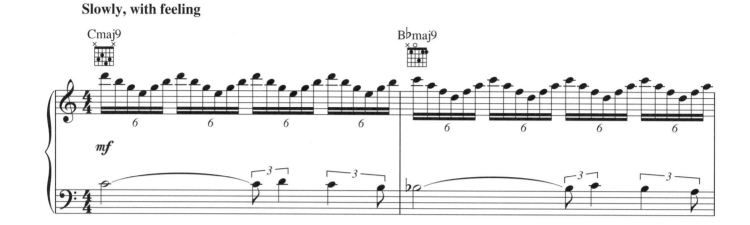

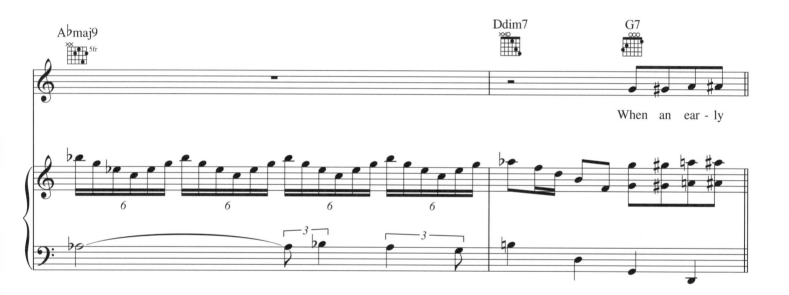

When an ear - ly

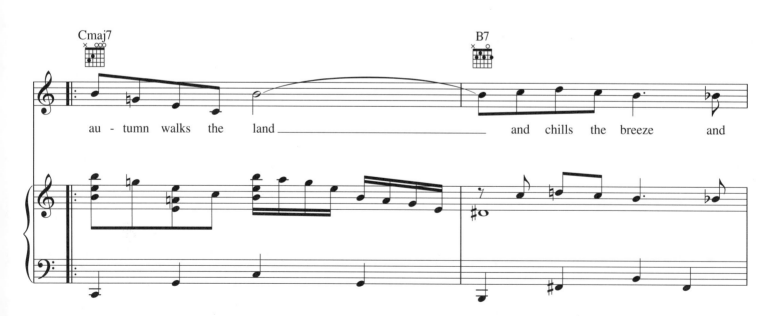

au - tumn walks the land _____ and chills the breeze and

EASY STREET

By ALAN RANKIN JONES

ENJOY YOURSELF
(It's Later Than You Think)

Lyric by HERB MAGIDSON
Music by CARL SIGMAN

EVERYTHING HAPPENS TO ME

Words by TOM ADAIR
Music by MATT DENNIS

FIVE MINUTES MORE

Lyric by SAMMY CAHN
Music by JULE STYNE

Moderately, with rhythm

Dear, this eve-ning seemed to go so aw-f'lly fast.____ We had so much fun and now you're home at last.____ I looked for-ward to a kiss or two at the gar-den gate,____ but you gave me just one

74

FOR EVERY MAN THERE'S A WOMAN

from the Motion Picture CASBAH

Lyric by LEO ROBIN
Music by HAROLD ARLEN

FOOLISH HEART
from the Musical Production ONE TOUCH OF VENUS

Words by OGDEN NASH
Music by KURT WEILL

FOR YOU, FOR ME, FOR EVERMORE

Music and Lyrics by GEORGE GERSHWIN
and IRA GERSHWIN

Par - a - dise can - not re - fuse us, Nev - er such a hap - py pair!

Ev - 'ry - bod - y must ex - cuse us

FRENESÍ

Words and Music by
ALBERTO DOMÍNGUEZ

HAUNTED HEART
from INSIDE U.S.A.

Words by HOWARD DIETZ
Music by ARTHUR SCHWARTZ

THE FRIM FRAM SAUCE

Words and Music by JOE RICARDEL
and REDD EVANS

HEY! BA-BA-RE-BOP

Words and Music by LIONEL HAMPTON
and CURLEY HAMMER

HOORAY FOR LOVE

from the Motion Picture CASBAH

Lyric by LEO ROBIN
Music by HAROLD ARLEN

HOW LITTLE WE KNOW

Words and Music by HOAGY CARMICHAEL
and JOHNNY MERCER

THE HUCKLEBUCK

Lyrics by ROY ALFRED
Music by ANDY GIBSON

Slow Blues tempo

THE HUT-SUT SONG

Words and Music by LEO V. KILLION,
TED MCMICHAEL and JACK OWENS

I AIN'T GOT NOTHIN' BUT THE BLUES

Words by DON GEORGE
Music by DUKE ELLINGTON

I HEAR MUSIC

from the Paramount Picture DANCING ON A DIME

Words by FRANK LOESSER
Music by BURTON LANE

I'LL NEVER SMILE AGAIN

Words and Music by
RUTH LOWE

I REMEMBER YOU

from the Paramount Picture THE FLEET'S IN

Words by JOHNNY MERCER
Music by VICTOR SCHERTZINGER

I WISH YOU LOVE

English Words by ALBERT BEACH
French Words and Music by CHARLES TRENET

IN LOVE IN VAIN

Words by LEO ROBIN
Music by JEROME KERN

Love can be a bless-ing, but al-so most de-press-ing, and I don't mind con-fess-ing that I feel might-y blue! It's on-ly hu-man for an-y-one to

IT'S A PITY TO SAY GOODNIGHT

Words and Music by
BILLY REID

Moderately, with a relaxed beat

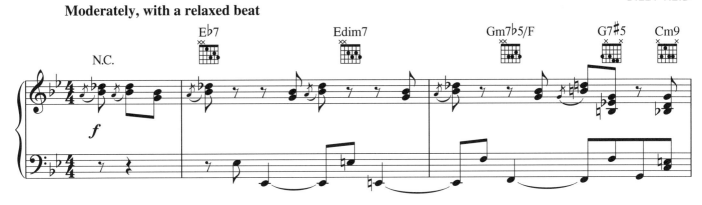

What a shame the

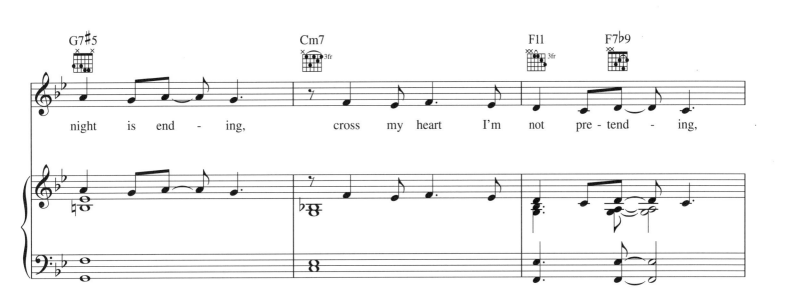

night is end - ing, cross my heart I'm not pre - tend - ing,

IT COULD HAPPEN TO YOU

from the Paramount Picture AND THE ANGELS SING

Words by JOHNNY BURKE
Music by JAMES VAN HEUSEN

IVY
from the Motion Picture IVY

Words and Music by
HOAGY CARMICHAEL

Slow and haunting

JUST SQUEEZE ME
(But Don't Tease Me)

Words by LEE GAINES
Music by DUKE ELLINGTON

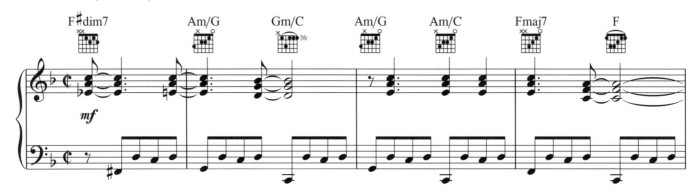

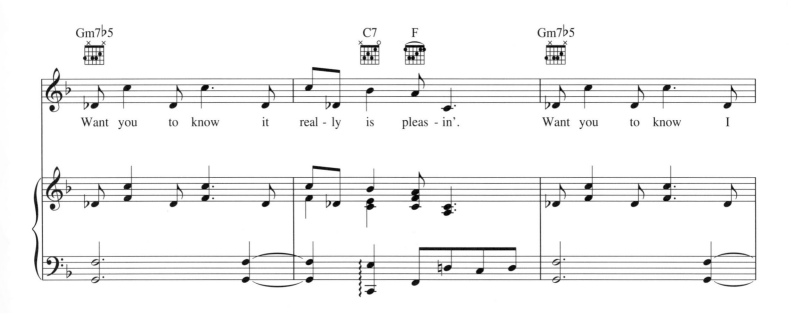

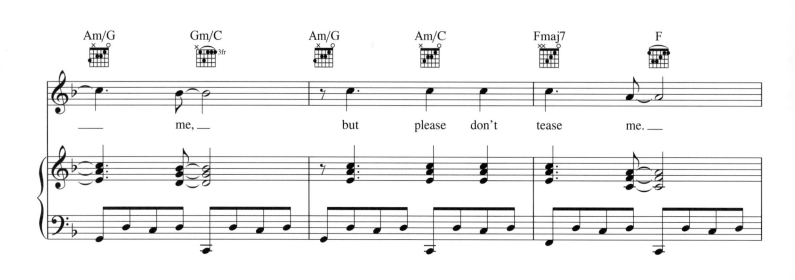

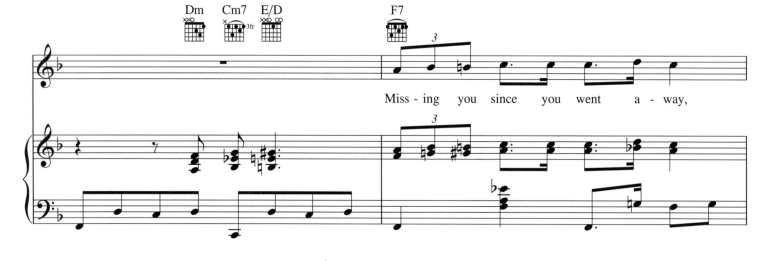

LET'S GET AWAY FROM IT ALL

Words and Music by TOM ADAIR
and MATT DENNIS

LIKE SOMEONE IN LOVE

Words by JOHNNY BURKE
Music by JIMMY VAN HEUSEN

LINDA

Words and Music by
JACK LAWRENCE

OLE BUTTERMILK SKY
from the Motion Picture CANYON PASSAGE

Words and Music by HOAGY CARMICHAEL
and JACK BROOKS

LOVE LETTERS
Theme from the Paramount Picture LOVE LETTERS

Words by EDWARD HEYMAN
Music by VICTOR YOUNG

The sky may be star - less, the night may be moon - less, but deep in my heart there's a glow, _____ for

ONCE IN LOVE WITH AMY

from WHERE'S CHARLEY?

By FRANK LOESSER

OPEN THE DOOR, RICHARD!

Words by "DUSTY" FLETCHER and JOHN MASON
Music by JACK McVEA and DAN HOWELL

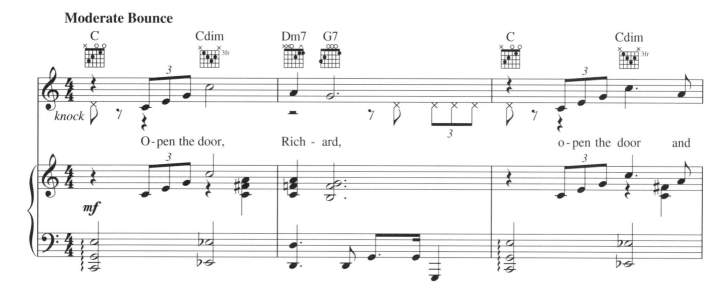

ONE DOZEN ROSES

Words by ROGER LEWIS and "COUNTRY" JOE WASHBURN
Music by DICK JURGENS and WALTER DONOVAN

SIOUX CITY SUE

Words by RAY FREEDMAN
Music by DICK THOMAS

SKYLARK

Words by JOHNNY MERCER
Music by HOAGY CARMICHAEL

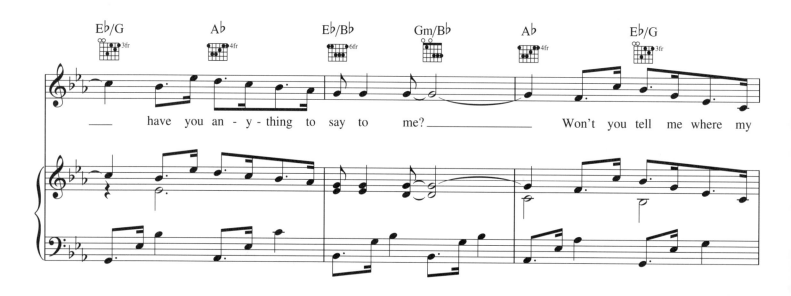

STEPPIN' OUT WITH MY BABY

from the Motion Picture Irving Berlin's EASTER PARADE

Words and Music by
IRVING BERLIN

TENDERLY
from TORCH SONG

Lyric by JACK LAWRENCE
Music by WALTER GROSS

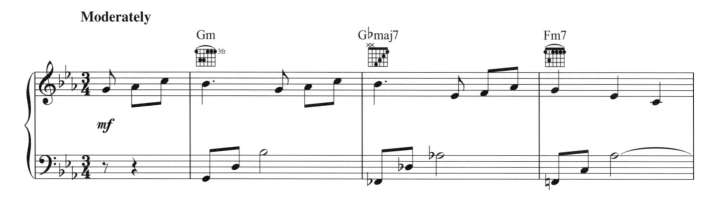

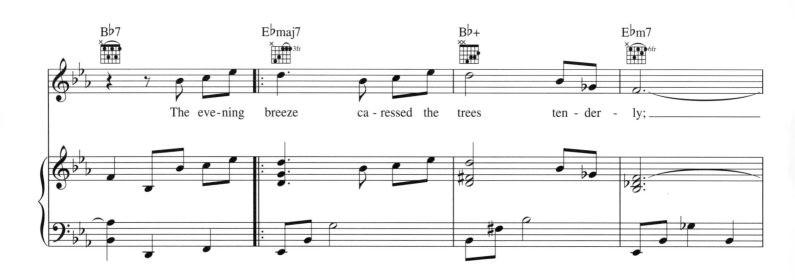

The eve-ning breeze ca-ressed the trees ten-der-ly;

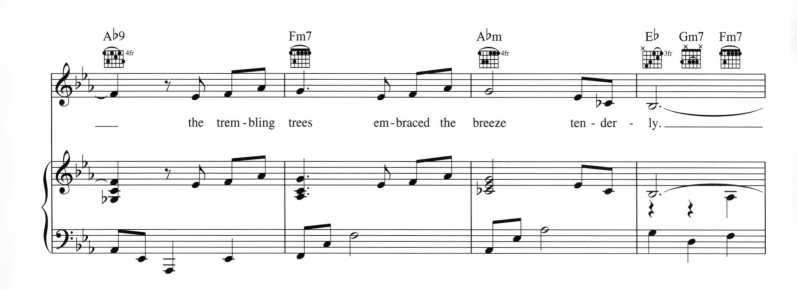

the trem-bling trees em-braced the breeze ten-der-ly.

THERE ARE SUCH THINGS

Words and Music by STANLEY ADAMS,
ABEL BAER and GEORGE W. MEYER

199

THERE! I'VE SAID IT AGAIN

Words and Music by DAVE MANN
and REDD EVANS

THERE WILL NEVER BE ANOTHER YOU

from the Motion Picture ICELAND

Lyric by MACK GORDON
Music by HARRY WARREN

Sweetly

This is our last dance to- geth- er, _____ to-

night soon will be long a- go. _____ And in our

mo- ment of part- ing, _____ this is all I

204

THEY SAY IT'S WONDERFUL
from the Stage Production ANNIE GET YOUR GUN

Words and Music by
IRVING BERLIN

TO EACH HIS OWN

from the Paramount Picture TO EACH HIS OWN
from the Paramount Picture THE CONVERSATION

Words and Music by JAY LIVINGSTON
and RAY EVANS

Lyrics:

Wise men have shown life is no good a-lone. Day needs night, flow-ers need light, I need you, I need

WHY DON'T YOU DO RIGHT
(Get Me Some Money, Too!)

By JOE McCOY

YOU DON'T KNOW WHAT LOVE IS

Words and Music by DON RAYE
and GENE DePAUL

YOU'RE NOBODY 'TIL SOMEBODY LOVES YOU

Words and Music by RUSS MORGAN,
LARRY STOCK and JAMES CAVANAUGH